AF375507

To my Father,

I admire your unwavering support, guidance, and strength for our family. This book is my dedication to your love and sacrifices.

Dedication Page

Written with Love

I am born with love,
I am truly a gift from Above.

Fatherhood is more than capability.
It is a rewarding responsibility.

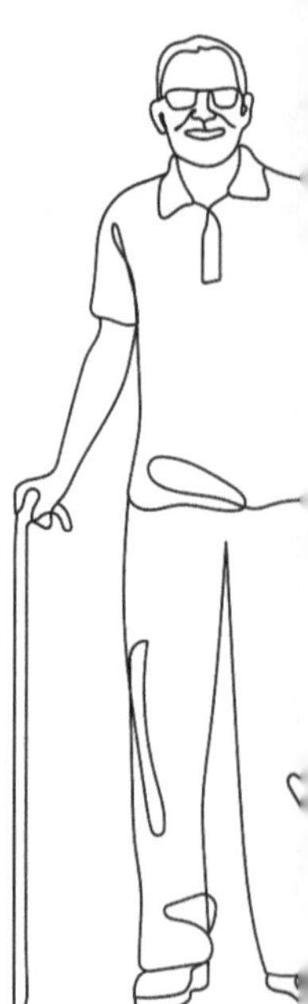

Thank you for your support and inspiration. **Dad**, you are my motivation.

HAPPY home Coming

I may have grown older and we may be apart. Yet, coming home is my favorite part.

Even when I am a
hundred miles away.
Your words will
forever stay.

I know I will be
guided by you,
with whatever in life
I will go through.

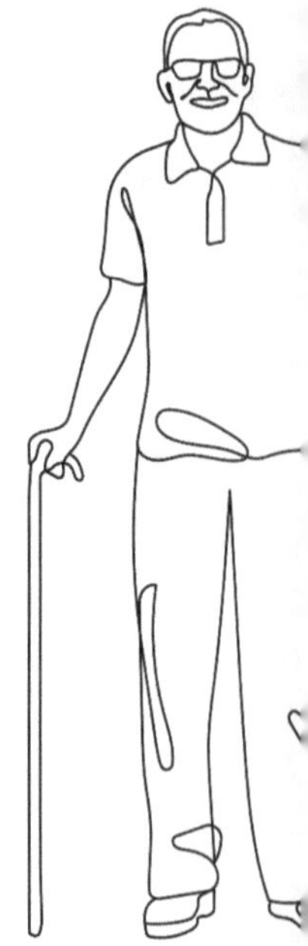

Think Positive

The lessons you taught
me,
I heeded carefully.

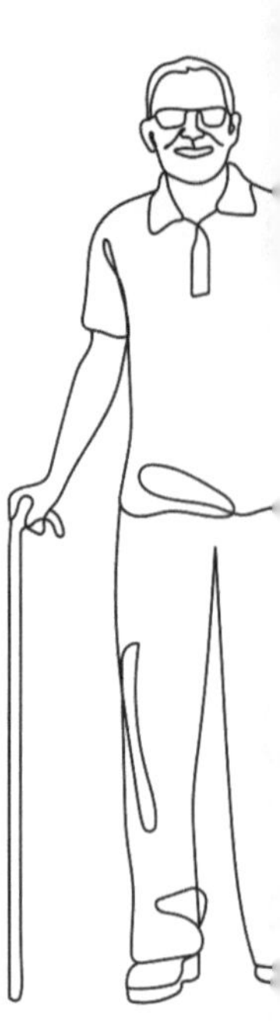

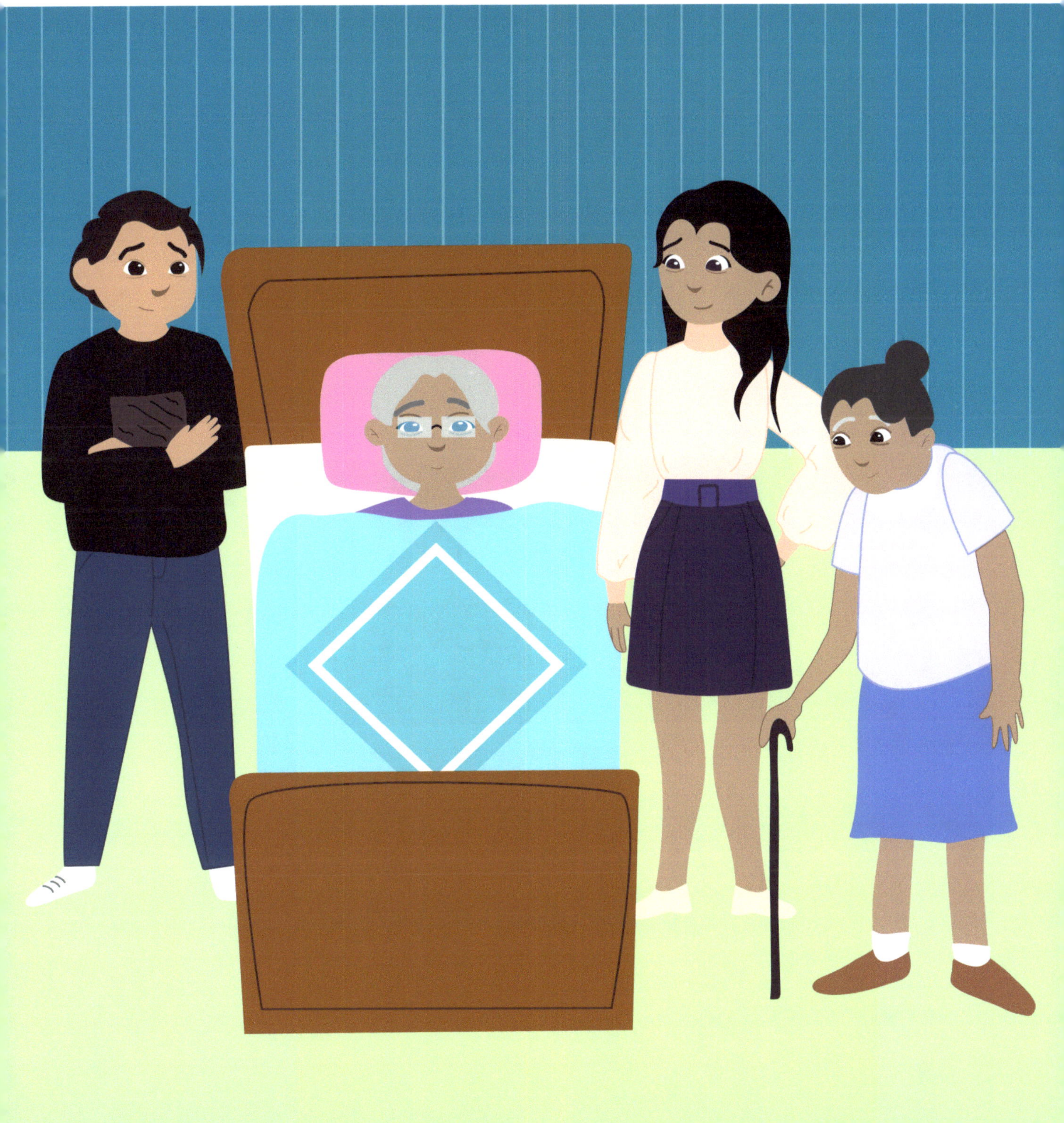

When you become
older and weaker,
I promise I will be
your power.

Dad, I am forever grateful for giving me a life so meaningful.

You serve as a foundation and our security.
Truly, You are the Pillar of our Home.